Instant HTML5 2D Platformer

Learn how to develop a 2D HTML5 platformer that is capable of running in modern browsers

Aidan Temple

BIRMINGHAM - MUMBAI

Instant HTML5 2D Platformer

First published: August 2013

Production Reference: 1230813

Published by Packt Publishing Ltd.
Livery Place
35 Livery Street
Birmingham B3 2PB, UK.

ISBN 978-1-84969-678-4

www.packtpub.com

Credits

Author

Aidan Temple

Reviewer

Ray Hammond

Acquisition Editor

Saleem Ahmed

Erol Staveley

Commissioning Editor

Priyanka S

Technical Editor

Sharvari H. Baet

Project Coordinator

Deenar Satam

Proofreader

Ting Baker

Production Coordinator

Prachali Bhiwandkar

Cover Work

Prachali Bhiwandkar

Cover Image

Disha Haria

About the Author

Aidan Temple is a software engineer and lead developer at Nanotek, an independent video game studio. He has recently graduated with honors from Glasgow Caledonian University where he studied BSc Computer Games Software Development.

During his time at university Aidan also undertook a research degree which outlined the possible benefits of implementing a GUI-based games framework by means of massively parallel processing through the utilization of Nvidia's CUDA architecture, which in turn successfully demonstrated the benefits of towards games development.. He also received one of the International Game Developers Associations most prestigious awards, an IGDA Scholarship which are awarded to exceptional students within the field of video games development.

Prior to his time at Glasgow Caledonian University, Aidan studied Computer Games Development at James Watt College of Further and Higher Education. Due to excellent understanding and demonstration of games development and design methodologies within a practical manner Aidan graduated from James Watt College with a distinction in his chosen field.

Without the help of my partner, Gemma, who kept me motivated and inspired, I would not have been able to undertake the work mentioned within this book.

Christina Donald for the art assets she created by giving up her spare time for the game, as well as those artists who offered their work for free on www.opengameart.org.

Without the help from Packt Publishing's staff, this book would not have been a reality. I would like to thank Priyanka Shah, Deenar Satam, and Sharvari Baet for helping to get the book off the ground.

I would also like to acknowledge each of the authors of various online articles as without their insight and knowledge in guiding me during development this book would not have been possible.

About the Reviewer

Ray Hammond is a software developer with over 15 years of experience in writing and reviewing code within the aviation industry. Ray has a passion for learning and runs a personal blog focusing on technologies such as HTML5, JavaScript, Linux, and security.

www.PacktPub.com

Support files, eBooks, discount offers and more

You might want to visit www.PacktPub.com for support files and downloads related to your book.

Did you know that Packt offers eBook versions of every book published, with PDF and ePub files available? You can upgrade to the eBook version at www.PacktPub.com and as a print book customer, you are entitled to a discount on the eBook copy. Get in touch with us at service@packtpub.com for more details.

At www.PacktPub.com, you can also read a collection of free technical articles, sign up for a range of free newsletters and receive exclusive discounts and offers on Packt books and eBooks.

http://PacktLib.PacktPub.com

Do you need instant solutions to your IT questions? PacktLib is Packt's online digital book library. Here, you can access, read and search across Packt's entire library of books.

Why subscribe?

- ▶ Fully searchable across every book published by Packt
- ▶ Copy and paste, print and bookmark content
- ▶ On demand and accessible via web browser

Free access for Packt account holders

If you have an account with Packt at www.PacktPub.com, you can use this to access PacktLib today and view nine entirely free books. Simply use your login credentials for immediate access.

Table of Contents

Preface

To begin with, the book will guide you through an introduction of the HTML5 canvas and some of the functionality that it provides to web and games developers. With an understanding of the HTML5 canvas, the book then gears its attention towards the creation of the 2D platform game in question by guiding you through the steps required to implement a basic game framework for any 2D HTML5 game.

The book will then progress iteratively through a number of components you might find within a 2D platform-based game. These components include monitoring and updating user input through means of a keyboard. Also covered are implementing a parallax background, adding enemies, and collectible items similar to the concept behind the coins in *Mario* and gold rings in *Sonic*. We will also look at implementing a basic form of physics, which will be used to allow the player to jump as well as introducing sound effects to the game to enhance its appeal.

What this book covers

Setting up your HTML5 canvas (Should know) gives an overview of how to set up the HTML5 canvas as well as some of the basic functionality the canvas has to offer and how we would go about implementing that functionality.

Implementing the game framework (Should know) is a step-by-step guide to the creation of a basic 2D game framework that takes advantage of polymorphism and which will be incrementally improved in each of the recipe. This framework will be responsible for updating and rendering game objects.

Creating the player (Must know) will look at the steps taken to implement a player class that will fit seamlessly with our game framework in order to load and draw the necessary assets to the canvas.

Handling user input (Must know) will improve upon the game framework introduced in an earlier task as well as enhance our player class to respond to the user's input. By responding to the user's input, we can move our player freely around the canvas.

Animating the player (Must know) will introduce an animation manager, which will allow us to load and render sprite sheet animations. We will also adjust the player class to take advantage of the animation manager so that we can animate the player.

Creating the level (Must know) will introduce a level class that will be responsible for loading and drawing a 2D tile-based level. With this level we can specify the layout of our level as well as the positioning of collectible items and the spawn locations of enemies.

Implementing a parallax background (Must know) will implement a new class, which will be responsible for drawing and updating each of the textures that make up the background. This updating will involve moving each of the background layers at differing speeds to produce a sense of depth within our game.

Implementing physics (Must know) explains how no game would be complete without some form of physics therefore we will implement this in the basic form of jumping. By introducing jumping we can implement more imaginative levels for the player to traverse as well as a means of avoiding enemy units.

Creating enemies (Must know) will improve upon the level class and implement an enemy class therefore allowing for the spawning of enemy units and updating their positions as they move around the level.

Adding pickups (Must know) will introduce the ability to collect items as a means of scoring points, which can also be a great way to compare your score with your friends.

Adding sounds (Must know) will look at implementing audio into our game that will be played each time the player collects an item or when the player take damage from an enemy.

Creating a graphical user interface (Must know) will draw a basic user interface to the canvas, which will be updated in real time to show the player's score and remaining health.

What you need for this book

As this book is intended to be used for the creation of a web-based game it is therefore necessary to have some form of text editor or an integrated development environment to work with. Readers who use a Microsoft-based operating system will be able to use Notepad whereas Mac readers will be able to use TextEdit. However, there are alternative development tools freely available online that are recommended rather than using a basic text editor. These tools include:

> ▸ Brackets is an open source editor for web design and development built on top of web technologies such as HTML, CSS, and JavaScript and is available for both Microsoft and Mac operating systems. (`www.brackets.io`)

- Notepad++ is a free to use open source code editor that supports several programming languages and that is a replacement for Microsoft's Notepad. (`www.notepad-plus-plus.org`)

- Aptana Studio is a complete integrated development environment for Microsoft, Mac, and Linux operating systems that include extensive capabilities for the creation of applications along with support for HTML, CSS, and JavaScript support. (`www.aptana.com`)

Who this book is for

This book has been written as a means of showing those with an interest in games development and who have a basic to intermediate understanding of the workings of HTML and JavaScript how to produce a 2D HTML5 platformer-based game. Therefore this book will not discuss the inner workings of either of these languages but will instead attempt to explain how the code within this book functions.

Conventions

In this book, you will find a number of styles of text that distinguish between different kinds of information. Here are some examples of these styles, and an explanation of their meaning.

Code words in text are shown as follows: " In order for our scripts to have any effect on our canvas we must create a separate file called `canvas example`."

A block of code is set as follows:

```
context.beginPath();
context.arc(350,150,40,0,2 * Math.PI);
context.stroke();
```

New terms and **important words** are shown in bold.

[Warnings or important notes appear in a box like this.]

[Tips and tricks appear like this.]

Reader feedback

Feedback from our readers is always welcome. Let us know what you think about this book—what you liked or may have disliked. Reader feedback is important for us to develop titles that you really get the most out of.

To send us general feedback, simply send an e-mail to feedback@packtpub.com, and mention the book title via the subject of your message.

If there is a topic that you have expertise in and you are interested in either writing or contributing to a book, see our author guide on www.packtpub.com/authors.

Customer support

Now that you are the proud owner of a Packt book, we have a number of things to help you to get the most from your purchase.

Downloading the example code

You can download the example code files for all Packt books you have purchased from your account at http://www.PacktPub.com. If you purchased this book elsewhere, you can visit http://www.PacktPub.com/support and register to have the files e-mailed directly to you.

Errata

Although we have taken every care to ensure the accuracy of our content, mistakes do happen. If you find a mistake in one of our books—maybe a mistake in the text or the code—we would be grateful if you would report this to us. By doing so, you can save other readers from frustration and help us improve subsequent versions of this book. If you find any errata, please report them by visiting http://www.packtpub.com/support, selecting your book, clicking on the **errata submission form** link, and entering the details of your errata. Once your errata are verified, your submission will be accepted and the errata will be uploaded on our website, or added to any list of existing errata, under the Errata section of that title. Any existing errata can be viewed by selecting your title from http://www.packtpub.com/support.

Piracy

Piracy of copyright material on the Internet is an ongoing problem across all media. At Packt, we take the protection of our copyright and licenses very seriously. If you come across any illegal copies of our works, in any form, on the Internet, please provide us with the location address or website name immediately so that we can pursue a remedy.

Please contact us at `copyright@packtpub.com` with a link to the suspected pirated material.

We appreciate your help in protecting our authors, and our ability to bring you valuable content.

Questions

You can contact us at `questions@packtpub.com` if you are having a problem with any aspect of the book, and we will do our best to address it.

Instant HTML5 2D Platformer

Welcome to *Instant HTML5 2D Platformer*. The purpose of this book is to outline the necessary steps taken in order to produce a 2D HTML5 Platformer, which is playable through a user's browser on their mobile or tablet device. In order to undertake the tasks within this book you must have a basic understanding of HTML and JavaScript as these will be the primary markup and programming languages used throughout the book.

Setting up your HTML5 canvas (Should know)

This recipe will show you how to first of all set up your own HTML5 canvas. With the canvas set up, we can then move on to look at some of the basic elements the canvas has to offer and how we would go about implementing them. For this task we will be creating a series of primitives such as circles and rectangles. Modern video games make use of these types of primitives in many different forms. For example, both circles and rectangles are commonly used within collision-detection algorithms such as bounding circles or bounding boxes.

How to do it...

As previously mentioned we will begin by creating our own HTML5 canvas.

1. We will start by creating a blank HTML file. To do this, you will need some form of text editor such as Microsoft Notepad (available for Windows) or the TextEdit application (available on Mac OS). Once you have a basic webpage set up, all that is left to do in order to create a canvas is to place the following between both body tags:

   ```
   <canvas id="canvas" width="800" height="600"></canvas>
   ```

2. As previously mentioned, we will be implementing a number of basic elements within the canvas. In order to do this we must first link the JavaScript file to our webpage. This file will be responsible for the initialization, loading, and drawing of objects to the canvas. In order for our scripts to have any effect on our canvas we must create a separate file called `canvas example`. Create this new file within your text editor and then insert the following code declarations:

```
var canvas = document.getElementById("canvas"), context = canvas.
getContext("2d");
```

3. These declarations are responsible for retrieving both the canvas element and context. Using the canvas context, we can begin to draw primitives, text, and load textures into our canvas. We will begin by drawing a rectangle in the top-left corner of our canvas. In order to do this place the following code below our previous JavaScript declarations:

```
context.fillStyle="#FF00FF";
context.fillRect(15,15,150,75);
```

4. If you were to now view the original webpage we created, you would see the rectangle being drawn in the top-left corner at position X: 15, Y: 15. Now that we have a rectangle, we can look at how we would go about drawing a circle onto our canvas. This can be achieved by means of the following code:

```
context.beginPath();
context.arc(350,150,40,0,2 * Math.PI);
context.stroke();
```

How it works...

The first code extract represents the basic framework required to produce a blank webpage and is necessary for a browser to read and display the webpage in question. With a basic webpage created, we then declare a new HTML5 canvas. This is done by assigning an `id` attribute, which we use to refer to the canvas within our scripts. The canvas declaration then takes a width and height attribute, both of which are also necessary to specify the size of the canvas, that is, the number of pixels wide and pixels high.

Before any objects can be drawn to the canvas, we first need to get the canvas element. This is done through means of the `getElementById` method that you can see in our canvas example. When retrieving the canvas element, we are also required to specify the canvas context by calling a built-in HTML5 method known as `getContext`. This object gives access to many different properties and methods for drawing edges, circles, rectangles, external images, and so on.

This can be seen when we draw a rectangle to our the canvas. This was done using the `fillStyle` property, which takes in a hexadecimal value and in return specifies the color of an element. Our next line makes use of the `fillRect` method, which requires a minimum of four values to be passed to it. These values include the X and Y position of the rectangle, as well as the width and height of the rectangle. As a result, a rectangle is drawn to the canvas with the color, position, width, and height specified.

We then move on to drawing a circle to the canvas, which is done by firstly calling a built-in HTML canvas method known as `BeginPath`. This method is used to either begin a new path or to reset a current path. With a new path setup, we then take advantage of a method known as `Arc` that allows for the creation of arcs or curves, which can be used to create circles. This method requires that we pass both an X and Y position, a radius, and a starting angle measured in radians. This angle is between 0 and 2 * Pi where 0 and 2 are located at the 3 o'clock position of the arc's circle. We also must pass an ending angle, which is also measured in radians. The following figure is taken directly from the W3C HTML canvas reference, which you can find at the following link `http://bit.ly/UCVPYl`:

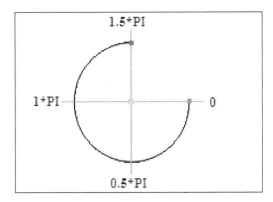

Implementing the game framework (Should know)

In this recipe, we will focus our attention on the creation of a basic 2D game framework through means of JavaScript and which will be added to throughout the remainder of the book. This framework will be responsible for declaring the size of the canvas as well as handling the loading, updating, and rendering of game assets.

How to do it...

1. In order to create a 2D game framework that will handle the initialization, updating, and rendering of assets, we must first of all start by creating a new blank HTML5 canvas by following the steps previously mentioned. Once you have created a blank canvas, we can then move onto creating the main JavaScript object responsible for initializing the application. Begin by creating a new JavaScript object entitled `Main` then input the following code into the `Main` object:

```
var frameTime = 0.0333;
var objectManager = null;

window.onload = function() {
   new ObjectManager().InitObjectManager();
}

function Main() {
    this.Initialise = function() {
        return this;
    };
}
```

The `main` object is responsible for kick-starting the application as well as determining the desired frame rate, which will be fundamental to the application.

2. Next we create a new object, which will be responsible for handling each of the objects within the game, that is, initializing and disposing of objects. Go ahead and insert the following code:

```
function Object() {

    this.x = 0;
    this.y = 0;
    this.z = 0;

    this.InitObject - function(x, y, z) {
        this.x = x;
        this.y = y;
        this.z = z;

        objectManager.AddObject(this);
        return this;
    }

    this.DisposeObject = function() {
        objectManager.RemoveObject(this);
    }
}
```

3. However, in order to make use of these objects and render them to the canvas, we will require an object that handles the drawing of game objects. For this we will create an object called `DrawableObject`. Once the object has been created, we can then move on to writing the contents of the object as follows:

```
function DrawableObject() {
    this.texture = null;

    this.InitDrawableObject = function(texture, x, y, z) {
        this.InitObject(x, y, z);
        this.texture = texture;
        return this;
    }

    this.Draw = function(deltaTime, context, deltaX, deltaY) {
        context.drawImage(this.texture, this.x - deltaX, this.y -
                          deltaY);
    }

    this.DisposeDrawableObject = function() {
        this.DisposeObject();
    }
}

DrawableObject.prototype = new Object;
```

4. We must now create the final object for our framework, which will be responsible for pulling together each of the previously created objects in a manageable way. By taking this approach, we are able to manage the loading and rendering of assets to the canvas. As we did earlier, we must create a new object called `ObjectManager`. `js`, which will first of all contain a number of variable declarations as well as initialize a new instance of `Main.js` and our canvas element.

```
function ObjectManager() {
    this.objects = new Array();
    this.terminalFrame = new Date().getTime();

    this.deltaX = 0;
    this.deltaY = 0;

    this.main = null;
    this.canvas = null;
    this.context = null;

    this.InitObjectManager = function() {
        objectManager = this;

        this.canvas = document.getElementById('canvas');
```

```
        this.context = this.canvas.getContext('2d');

        this.main = new Main().Initialise();
        setInterval(function() {objectManager.Draw();},
                    frameTime);
        return this;
    }
```

5. With the canvas element initialized, we can then move on to adding objects to the application. This is achieved by pushing a number of items to the previously declared array of objects, which can be seen in the preceding code. We will also look at how to remove these objects once we are finished with them.

```
    this.AddObject = function(Object) {
        this.objects.push(Object);
        this.objects.sort(function(a,b){return a.z - b.z;})
    };

    this.RemoveObject = function(object) {

        for (var i = 0; i < this.length; ++i) {

        if (this[i] === object) {
            this.remove(i);
            break;
        }
        }
    }
```

6. You can see that we are attempting to remove an item from our objects array. However, to do this, we must first add a new function to JavaScript's built-in array object.

```
Array.prototype.remove = function (a, b) {
    var rest = this.slice((b || a) + 1 || this.length);

    if(a < 0)
        this.length + a;
    else
        this.length = a;

    return this.push.apply(this, rest);
};
```

7. Now that we can add and remove objects to our framework, we can move on to our final part of the framework, drawing objects to our canvas. This is done by clearing the canvas and then drawing each object to it every time the `Draw` function is called.

```
this.Draw = function () {
        var frame = new Date().getTime();
```

```
        var deltaTime = (frame - this.terminalFrame) / 1000;
        this.terminalFrame = frame;

        this.context.clearRect(0, 0, this.canvas.width, this.
                            canvas.height);

    for (obj in this.objects) {

    if (this.objects[obj].Draw) {
    this.objects[obj].Draw(deltaTime, this.context, this.deltaX, this.
    deltaY);
            }

    this.context.drawImage(this.canvas, 0, 0);
    };
```

How it works...

The first object we created is responsible for executing the application. Within this object, a number of variables are declared that are responsible for creating a new instance of the object manager as well as the time it takes to update each frame per second. The execution of the application is done firstly by loading the HTML file. Once loaded, the onload function within Main is called, and as a result a new object manager is initialized.

The object script within the framework is responsible for initializing a new game object such as a player sprite, or level tile. These objects consist of a series of components that represent the x, y, and z positions of an object on the screen. As we are creating a 2D game the z coordinate represents the draw order of objects, for example, if an object has a z value of zero then that object would be drawn in front of all others thus giving the illusion of depth.

The last object within our game framework is used to load a texture that will represent a game object and then draw that texture to the canvas. This object also has access to the methods and properties of the object and as a result each drawable object is drawn to the positions passed to it via the object script.

Drawing objects to the canvas is achieved through means of the Draw function within the object manager. This function begins by clearing all objects from the canvas and then updating the next frame and drawing this frame to the canvas. This is done at a rate of 30 frames per second.

Scope then jumps to the object manager constructor, which firstly begins by initializing a number of variables related to the canvas and its context. It also gives a call to update the `Draw` function of the application at 30 frames per second. The constructor then makes a call to the `Main` constructor, which initializes and draws all game objects to the screen. However, in this instance we do not have any game objects to draw to the canvas.

The remainder of the object manager is responsible for adding and removing game objects to an array of objects that are later updated and drawn to the canvas.

Creating the player (Must know)

With a basic game framework in place, we can start by developing an object that will handle the player and any behaviors they may have. This will involve expanding upon the game framework to handle the loading of a sprite, which will be used to represent the player within the game.

How to do it...

1. We must first begin by creating a new object called `Player`. Once created, insert the following code into our `player` object. This object is responsible for initializing and drawing the player on the canvas as well as stating the players position on the canvas.

   ```
   function Player() {
       this.InitPlayer = function() {

           this.InitDrawableObject(player_idle, 0, 0, 0);
           return this;
       }
   }


   Player.prototype = new DrawableObject;
   ```

2. With our `player` object completed, we then need to load the sprite texture into our application. In order to do this, we need to edit the `Main.js` object we created previously, open `Main.js` and before the `Onload` function we will declare a new image object, which will be used to hold our sprite texture.

   ```
   var player_idle = new Image();
   player_idle.src = "idle_left.png";
   ```

3. The final step is to initialize our player object by calling the `player` constructor and passing the player sprite to it.

   ```
   this.player = new Player().InitPlayer(player_idle);
   ```

4. If we were to open the application's HTML file in any modern browser we would see the player sprite drawn in the top-left corner of the canvas.

How it works...

When creating a new game object, in this case the `player` object, we must first create a new image object within the `Main` object and then assign an external path to the object by setting the source property. In return this results in a texture being loaded into our application that is the player sprite texture. This texture is then passed to the player object and is assigned a position and draw order on the canvas; this is done by means of the drawable object script. In return, the constructor within `Main` is passed the player sprite and initializes a new player object, which then draws the player sprite to the canvas.

Handling user input (Must know)

This task will outline and demonstrate the necessary steps required to handle the keyboard input in order to move the player sprite around the canvas. This will be done by looking at how to handle different states of any given key on the keyboard and updating the players position each frame by modifying both the `Player` and `ObjectManager` objects in order to do so.

How to do it...

1. To support keyboard input within our application, we firstly need to modify the player object to monitor the state of each key pressed as well as updating the position of the player in each frame.

2. To begin with, we will outline a series of variables that will be used to determine the velocity of the player, that is, the direction and speed at which the player is moving.

    ```
    this.velocity = 50;
    this.up = false;
    this.down = false;
    this.left = false;
    this.right = false;
    ```

3. Next we will create two functions, which are used to determine whether or not a key has been pressed or released. More specifically, we will determine the state of each of the arrow keys as well as the *W, A, S, D* keys.

    ```
    this.keyDown = function(key) {

    if (key.keyCode == 38 || key.keyCode == 87)
    this.up = true;

    if (key.keyCode == 40 || key.keyCode == 83)
    this.down = true;

    if (key.keyCode == 37 || key.keyCode == 65)
    ```

```
        this.left = true;

        if (key.keyCode == 39 || key.keyCode == 68)
        this.right = true;
        }


        this.keyUp = function(key) {

        if (key.keyCode == 38 || key.keyCode == 87)
        this.up = false;

        if (key.keyCode == 40 || key.keyCode == 83)
        this.down = false;

        if (key.keyCode == 37 || key.keyCode == 65)
        this.left = false;

        if (key.keyCode == 39 || key.keyCode == 68)
        this.right = false;
        }
```

4. Each of these functions performs a number of checks to determine whether a key has been pressed or released. As a result these checks determine in which direction the player should move if a certain key has been pressed.

5. In order to move the player in the direction in question, we must update the number of units the player has moved each frame by introducing an `Update` function to the player object as follows:

```
this.Update = function (deltaTime, context, deltaX, deltaY) {

if(this.up)
this.y -= this.velocity * deltaTime;

if(this.down)
this.y += this.velocity * deltaTime;

if (this.left)
this.x -= this.velocity * deltaTime;

if (this.right)
this.x += this.velocity * deltaTime;
}
```

6. The next step required is to initialize keyboard input and call both the KeyDown and KeyUp events inside of the InitObjectManager constructor as follows:

```
document.onkeydown = function(key){objectManager.keyDown(key);}
document.onkeyup = function(key){objectManager.keyUp(key);}
```

7. Once a key is pressed, each of the previously declared events trigger one of two corresponding functions, which we will now declare below the InitObjectManager constructor.

```
this.keyDown = function(event) {

for (obj in this.objects) {
            if (this.objects[obj].keyDown)
    this.objects[obj].keyDown(event);
}
}


this.keyUp = function(event) {

for (obj in this.objects) {
            if (this.objects[obj].keyUp)
    this.objects[obj].keyUp(event);
}
}
```

8. The final step required is to modify the object manager's Draw function. Replace the *for* loop within our Draw function with the modified loop as follows:

```
for (obj in this.objects) {

if (this.objects[obj].Update) {
this.objects[obj].Update(deltaTime, this.context, this.deltaX,
this.deltaY);
}

if (this.objects[obj].Draw) {
this.objects[obj].Draw(deltaTime, this.context, this.deltaX, this.
deltaY);
}
}
```

How it works...

In order to move the player, we first began by declaring the velocity, which includes the speed or pixels the player moves per frame. This velocity also includes the direction in which the player moves, that is, up, down, left, or right. Each direction is a Boolean value and is initially set to `false`.

In order to determine whether or not the player wishes to move in one of these four directions we then implemented two functions. Each of which determines the state of a given key on the keyboard.

This is done through means of the `KeyDown` and `KeyUp` functions declared within the `Player` object. Both of these functions determine if any of the arrow keys or the *W*, *A*, *S*, or *D* keys have previously been pressed or released. As a result, the `KeyDown` function returns `true` if a key has been pressed and the `KeyUp` function returns `false` if no key is being pressed. More information on key numbering or a list of ASCII and JavaScript key codes can be found at the website `http://bit.ly/tuzd3s`.

We then implemented an `Update` function within the `player` object, which moves the player in the direction determined by the Boolean variables previously declared. This `update` function is called within the `draw` function of the object manager object. These directional values correspond to a key press, that is, if the up arrow key is pressed the up value returns `true` and the `Update` function moves the player sprite 50 pixels up the canvas and similarly for the down, left, and right directional values.

In order to determine if the player has pressed or released a key we must first implement a prebuilt JavaScript event for each of these states. This is achieved through the `onkeydown` and `onkeyup` event handlers within our object manager object.

Each of these event handlers call their corresponding `KeyDown` and `KeyUp` functions. These functions are also declared within the object manager object and are used to loop through each game object and in return call the `KeyDown` and `KeyUp` functions within the player object. In order to see the player sprite moving on the screen, we then finally implement a call to update and draw each game object 30 times a second.

Animating the player (Must know)

For this task, we will focus on enhancing the visual appeal of the game by introducing and demonstrating the necessary steps required to animate the player sprite. These steps will involve adjusting the game framework to handle the loading and updating animated sprite sheets.

How to do it...

1. To begin with, we must introduce a new object to the games framework. This object will be responsible for animating the player sprite through means of a sprite sheet.

2. Create a new object called `AnimationManager`. With the animation object open, copy the following code in it:

```
function AnimationManager() {

    this.currentFrame = 0;
    this.frameRate = 0;
    this.frameTime = 0;
    this.frameWidth = 0;
this.frameHeight = 0;

    this.InitAnimationManager = function(texture, x, y, z,
frameCount, framesPerSec) {

        this.InitDrawableObject(texture, x, y, z);
        this.currentFrame = 0;
        this.frameCount = frameCount;
        this.frameRate = 1 / framesPerSec;
        this.frameTime = this.frameRate;
        this.frameWidth = this.texture.width / this.frameCount;
  this.frameHeight = this.texture.height;

        return this;
    }

this.Draw = function(deltaTime, context, deltaX, deltaY) {

var sourceRect = this.frameWidth * this.currentFrame;
context.drawImage(this.texture, sourceRect, 0,
  this.frameWidth,  this.frameHeight, this.x - deltaX,
  this.y - deltaY,  this.frameWidth, this.frameHeight);

this.frameTime -= deltaTime;

if (this.frameTime <= 0)
{
this.frameTime = this.frameRate;
++this.currentFrame;
this.currentFrame %= this.frameCount;
}
}
}

AnimationManager.prototype = new DrawableObject;
```

3. The next step is to modify the call to initialize the drawing of the player sprite. Inside of the `Player` object constructor replace the `InitDrawableObject` call with the following:

```
this.InitAnimationManager(player_idle_left, 300, 300, 1, 6, 20);
```

4. Similarly replace the prototype property at the bottom of the player object with the following:

```
Player.prototype = new AnimationManager;
```

5. The final step is to replace the player sprite with the sprite sheet animation, which can be found within the `Chapter 1 Task 5 images` folder provided with the book. If you run the application you should see an animated player sprite in the top-left corner of the application.

How it works...

The animation manager is an extension of the drawable object we created previously and as a result introduces an additional `draw` function that is able to output animated sprites. The animation manager begins by declaring a number of variables that relate to the frame rate of the given sprite, the time taken to animate the sprite as well as the width and height of a given frame within a sprite sheet.

Each of these variables is initialized within the `InitAnimationManager` constructor. The animation manager constructor also takes in a texture, that is, a sprite sheet, a 2D position, and a depth variable used to determine the drawing order of objects.

The `draw` method within the animation manager is responsible for creating a source rectangle, which is positioned above the first cell in the sprite sheet. For each frame the source rectangle is positioned above the next cell within the sprite sheet. Once the source rectangle reaches the end of the sprite sheet its position is reset to the first cell. By doing this we are selectively picking out and displaying one cell at a time from the sprite sheet. We then loop through each cell at a frame rate, which gives the illusion of animation, in this case 12 frames per second.

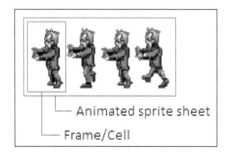

Animated sprite sheet

Frame/Cell

In order to display an animated sprite on the canvas, we replaced the call to initialize drawing of the player sprite within the player constructor. Previously, we passed the player texture and position to the `DrawableObject` constructor. However, now that we are animating the player we also need to pass a frame count and frame rate, that is, the number of cells within the sprite sheet and the rate at which the animation is updated per second. Finally, we use the prototype keyword to extend the functionality of the `DrawableObject` constructor to the `AnimationManager` function.

Creating the level (Must know)

In this recipe, we will look at the necessary steps required to create and implement a level. This will be done by implementing a level object and updating the games framework to handle the loading and drawing of modular 2D tile assets. This modular construction allows levels to be designed with varying environmental layouts and sizes.

How to do it...

1. In order to implement a level, we will need to modify both the `Player` and `Main` objects as well as introduce a level manager object. Go ahead and open the `Main` object and add the following declaration below where we declared and loaded our player sprite:

   ```
   var tile = new Image();
   tile.src = "textures/tile.png";
   ```

2. This declaration creates a new image object, which will represent the terrain within the level as well as the path to the tiles texture. Next we will initialize a new instance of the level object we are yet to make as well as passing the level to our player object. Modify the contents of the `Initialise` function in our `Main` object as follows:

   ```
   this.level = new Level().InitLevel();
   this.player = new Player().InitPlayer(this.level);
   ```

3. Next we will need to modify the `Player` object, which will be responsible for initializing the level and for performing any collision detection to determine if the player is standing on the terrain and whether or not the player has collided with any obstacles in the player's path. Insert the following variables into the `Player` object and then modify the `Player` constructor in order to retrieve and initialize a level object:

   ```
   this.level = null;

   this.InitPlayer = function(level) {
   this.InitAnimationManager(player_idle_left, 300, 600 - 48 - 48, 4,
   6, 20);
   this.level = level;
        return this;
   }
   ```

4. The next stage is to implement some form of collision detection to determine whether or not the player is standing on the terrain or has collided with an obstacle. To do this we will modify the `Update` function within the `Player` object. Insert the following below the code that moves the player in a given direction:

```
var collision, position, curTile, terrainHeight, playerHeight;

if ((this.right || this.left) && !(this.left && this.right)) {

collision = false;

do {
position = this.left ? this.x : this.x + this.frameWidth;
curTile = this.level.CurrentTile(position);
terrainHeight = this.level.TerrainHeight(curTile);
playerHeight = context.canvas.height - (this.y + this.texture.
height);

if (playerHeight  < terrainHeight) {
collision = true;

                         if (this.right)
this.x = this.level.tileWidth * curTile - this.frameWidth - 1;
else
this.x = this.level.tileWidth * (curTile + 1);
}
else
collision = false;
} while (collision)
}
```

5. The final step is to implement the `Level` object. Create the `Level` object and insert the following code in it:

```
function Level() {

    this.tiles = new Array();
    this.tileWidth = 0;
    this.tileHeight = 0;

    this.InitLevel = function() {
  this.tileWidth = tile.width;
  this.tileHeight = tile.height;

  for(var i = 0; i < 50; i++) {
        this.tiles[i] = 1;
  }
```

```
        this.AddTiles();
        return this;
    };

    this.AddTiles = function() {
        for (var x = 0; x < this.tiles.length; ++x) {
            for (var y = 0; y < this.tiles[x]; ++y)
                new DrawableObject().InitDrawableObject(tile, x *
                this.tileWidth, 600 - (y + 1) * this.tileHeight, 4);
        }
    };

    this.CurrentTile = function(x) {
        return parseInt( x / this.tileWidth);
    };

    this.TerrainHeight = function(index) {
        if (index < 0 || index > this.tiles.length)
        return 0;

        return this.tiles[index] *  this.tileHeight;
    };
}
```

How it works...

We first start off by creating a new image object within the `Main` object. This object represents a 2D tile module that the level is made up of. Similarly, to the player sprite this object loads an external texture into the application. We then declare and initialize a new instance of the `Level` object. This `Level` object is also passed into the `Player` constructor so that it can be accessed and utilized within the `Player` object.

Within the `Player` object, we then assign a reference to the level object, passed into the `Player` constructor, to a local level object. This reference is used to check whether or not the player is intersecting the levels terrain.

These collision detection checks are only employed when the player chooses to move left or right. When moving in either direction if the player collides with an obstacle they are pushed back to the point of intersection thus preventing them from passing through an obstacle.

The level object itself is made up of a constructor and a number of helper functions that are used to add tile modules into the level thus dictate the layout of the environment. The object also contains helper functions that are used to determine if the player is colliding with the terrain in their current position as well as a function for checking the height for each stack of tiles.

The constructor of the level object initializes the width and height of the tiles passed into it. This is done by retrieving the width and height of the tile image object that was previously loaded into the application, inside of the main object. The remainder of the constructor is used to determine the height of each stack of terrain tiles as well as how many stacks make up the level's terrain.

Each of these stacks of tiles are stored within an array that is passed into the `AddTiles` function within the `Level` object. This array is then looped through and each tile within a stack drawn on top of each other and each stack drawn next to the previous stack thus resulting a 2D terrain the player can interact with.

Implementing a parallax background (Must know)

In this recipe, we will implement a parallax effect for the game's background images. This effect causes the background to move at a slower rate than the foreground, which in return helps to give the illusion of depth within our game. More specifically this technique is achieved by placing multiple layers in front of each other and moving them at different speeds along the x axis.

How to do it...

1. To do this, we will need to implement a new object called `ScrollingBackground` with the following code:

```
function ScrollingBackground() {

    this.width = 0;
    this.height = 0;
    this.deltaScroll = 1;

    this.InitScrollingBackground = function(texture, x, y, z,
                                    width, height, deltaScroll) {

        this.InitDrawableObject(texture, x, y, z);
        this.width = width;
        this.height = height;
        this.deltaScroll = deltaScroll;

        return this;
    }

    this.DisposeScrollingBackground = function() {
        this.DisposeDrawableObject();
    };
```

```
this.UpdateBackground = function(canvas, position, fillArea,
deltaPosition) {

  var left;
  var top;
  var width;
  var height;

   var xOffset = Math.abs(deltaPosition[0]) % this.texture.width;
   var yOffset = Math.abs(deltaPosition[1]) % this.texture.height;

if(deltaPosition[0] < 0)
left = this.texture.width - xOffset;
else
left = xOffset;

if(deltaPosition[1] < 0)
top = this.texture.height - yOffset;
else
top = yOffset;

if(fillArea[0] < this.texture.width - left)
width = fillArea[0];
else
width = this.texture.width - left;

if(fillArea[1] < this.texture.height - top)
height = fillArea[1];
else
  height = this.texture.height - top;

      canvas.drawImage(this.texture, left, top, width, height,
                    position[0], position[1], width, height);
        return [width, height];
    }

var background, position, fillArea, deltaPosition;

this.Draw = function(deltaTime, canvas, deltaX, deltaY) {
        background = [0, 0];

        for (var y = 0; y < this.height; y += background[1]) {
            for (var x = 0; x < this.width; x += background[0]) {

            position = [this.x + x, this.y + y];
                fillArea = [this.width - x, this.height - y];
                deltaPosition = [0, 0];
```

```
if (x === 0)
{
[0] = deltaX * this.deltaScroll;
}

if (y === 0)
{
deltaPosition[1] = deltaY * this.deltaScroll;
}

background = this.UpdateBackground(canvas, position, fillArea,
deltaPosition);
            }
        }
      }
}

ScrollingBackground.prototype = new DrawableObject();
```

2. Before we can take advantage of this new object, we need to load the textures that will represent the background into our application.

```
var sky = new Image();
sky.src = "textures/sky.png";

var cloud = new Image();
cloud.src = "textures/cloud.png";

var mountain = new Image();
mountain.src = "textures/mountain.png";

var forest = new Image();
forest.src = "textures/forest.png";
```

3. With the `ScrollingBackground` object implemented and the required textures loaded, we then need to create a number of new instances of this object. Each of which will utilize the previously loaded textures that will be used to represent a layer within the background.

```
this.sky = new ScrollingBackground().InitScrollingBackground(sky,
0, 0, 1, 800, 600, 0.5);
this.cloud = new ScrollingBackground().
InitScrollingBackground(cloud, 0, 0, 2, 800, 600, 0.5);
this.mountain = new ScrollingBackground().InitScrollingBackground(
mountain, 0, 0, 3, 800, 600, 0.75);
this.forest = new ScrollingBackground().
InitScrollingBackground(forest, 0, 0, 4, 800, 600, 0.9);
```

4. With each of the background layers implemented and positioned correctly our level should look similar to the following screenshot:

How it works...

We begin by creating a new object called `ScrollingBackground`, which is responsible for moving a 2D texture horizontally along the canvas. Using a series of scrolling layers we are able to produce a parallax effect that gives off the illusion of depth within the game. This is achieved by moving the background layer(s) at a slower speed than those layers that are closer to the foreground. As each layer moves off the canvas it then wraps back around to the other side of the canvas thus continually looping. This is beneficial to game development as it helps to reduce the amount of assets required for level design. It can also be said that it is more efficient than loading large textures into our application, which would result in a decrease in performance.

The object in question requires that we pass a texture, 2D position, depth position, width, height, and speed to it. The texture parameter refers to the texture that is loaded into the application and that will be used to represent a background layer. The 2D position indicates where the texture should start to be drawn on the canvas, for example, the top-left corner of the canvas, whereas the depth position indicates the position of the texture within the list of layers that make up the game. The width and height are used to find the point at which the texture should be drawn to, that is its end point. The width and height parameters can be used to draw a portion of a texture rather than the whole texture thus increasing the overall performance of the application.

Finally the speed parameter is used to indicate how fast the texture should move along the x axis. This movement is also determined by the `deltaX` and `deltaY` variables within the `ScrollingBackground` object. Both of which are passed to the `Draw` and `Update` functions of the application and used to determine how far the texture has moved along the x axis. By knowing how far the texture has moved, we then know when to wrap the texture around the canvas using the `UpdateBackground` function. This function wraps the texture so that it is drawn on the right-hand side of the canvas, giving the illusion of a continually looping background.

With the `ScrollingBackground` object implemented, we then loaded each of the background layers into the application. This is done in much the same way as we have done in previous recipes. We declare a new image object and pass it the path of a texture for it to load into the application. A reference of this texture is then passed to a new instance of `ScrollingBackground`.

As well as passing a texture, we also pass a 2D position, depth position, width, height, and a speed with which the texture should move. This creates a new background layer, which is drawn to the canvas and placed behind the level. This process is repeated a number of times and as a result creates a series of background layers, each of which differ in speed and help to produce a parallax effect.

Implementing physics (Must know)

In this recipe, we will look at implementing a jumping behavior for the player. In order to implement this feature, we will need to adjust that section of the game framework, which is responsible for detecting and updating user input. By doing this, we can determine when the player has pressed either the *Space bar* key, the *W* key, or the up arrow key in order to make the player jump.

How to do it...

1. In order to implement jumping behavior, we will need to implement additional behaviors within the `Player` object. Open this object and declare the following variables at the top of the object:

    ```
    this.maxJump = 64;
    this.jumpTime = 1;
    this.jumpVelocity = ((Math.PI / 2) / this.jumpTime);
    this.position = 0;
    this.terminalVelocity = 1.5;
    this.isOnGround = true;
    ```

    These variables are responsible for the characteristics of the jump behaviors and they also determine the maximum height the player can jump, the time taken, the speed and trajectory of the jump, deceleration, and whether or not the player is on the ground before jump they can jump.

2. The next stage is to determine whether or not the user has pressed either the *Space bar* key, the *W* key, or the up arrow key. This is done in the same way as we detected the user input in previous recipes. We also need to check whether or not the player is on the ground and if they are only then can we allow them to jump.

```
if((key.keyCode == 32 || key.keyCode == 38 || key.keyCode == 87)
&& this.isOnGround) {
this.isOnGround = false
this.position = 0;
}
```

3. Next, we need to implement a check to see if the player is jumping and if so their position and speed needs to be updated until they have collided with the ground.

```
if(!this.isOnGround) {
var prevPosition = this.position;
this.position += this.jumpVelocity * deltaTime;

if(this.position >= Math.PI) {
  this.y += this.maxJump / this.jumpTime * this.terminalVelocity *
          deltaTime;
}
  else {
    this.y -= (Math.sin(this.position) - Math.sin(prevPosition)) *
this.maxJump;
  }
}
```

4. We then need to check if and when the player has collided with the levels terrain, if so then we change the player's ground state to `true`. If the player has not collided with the terrain we update the player's jump height and speed.

```
var checkCollisionLeft = this.level.CurrentTile(this.x);
var checkCollisionRight = this.level.CurrentTile(this.x + this.
frameWidth);

var heightLeft = this.level.TerrainHeight(checkCollisionLeft);
var heightRight = this.level.TerrainHeight(checkCollisionRight);
var maxHeight;

if(heightLeft > heightRight)
maxHeight = heightLeft
else
maxHeight = heightRight;

var playerHeight = context.canvas.height - (this.y + this.texture.
height);

if(maxHeight >= playerHeight) {
```

```
this.y = (context.canvas.height - maxHeight - this.texture.
height);
   this.isOnGround = true;
   this.position = 0;
}
else if(this.isOnGround) {
this.isOnGround = false;
this.position = (Math.PI / 2);
}
```

How it works...

We start off by declaring a number of variables that are used to reflect the player's behavior when jumping. These variables include the maximum jump height, time taken to jump, the speed and direction of the jump, as well as a Boolean variable that checks whether or not the player is on the ground.

The next step we took was to determine whether the user had pressed the *Space bar* key, the *W* key, or the up arrow key. If the player has pressed either of these keys and is on the ground then the player begins to jump. Depending on the keys pressed during the jump, the player will either jump straight up and return to its initial position or will jump and follow the path of a sine wave.

When the player reaches the peak of the wave then they will begin to decelerate at a speed of his/her initial jump speed multiplied by the terminal velocity value previously declared. This can be seen in the next recipe which employs a series of checks to determine whether the player is not on the ground, if so then we check where on the path of the sine wave the player is. The player's speed and position are then updated to reflect the player's position in the air.

Finally, we then employ a number of statements that are used to check if the player has collided with the terrain. Each of these collision detection statements check whether the left-hand side or right-hand side of the player has collided with the terrain. If the player has collided with the terrain, we change the `IsOnGround` Boolean variable to `true`. However if the player is not on the ground and was previously on the ground then they are falling and their speed and position is adjusted accordingly until grounded.

Creating enemies (Must know)

In this section, we will outline the steps taken to implement a number of animated enemy sprites that the player must attempt to avoid in order to stay alive. We will also look at the steps taken to implement a simplistic form of artificial intelligence known as patrolling. By utilizing this technique, we can give life to each of the enemies by allowing them to move freely around the level. This will involve the implementation of an `Enemy` object as well as adjusting the `Level` and `Main` objects to handle the newly created `Enemy` objects.

How to do it...

1. To begin with, we will implement the `Enemy` object, which will be responsible for creating and drawing enemies to the canvas. We will also be updating the enemy's position and performing collision detection.

```
function Enemy() {

    this.velocity = 30;

    this.InitEnemy = function(texture, x, y, z, frameCount,
                    frameRate) {
        this.InitAnimationManager(texture, x, y, z, frameCount,
        frameRate);

        return this;
    }

this.DisposeEnemy = function() {
        this.DisposeAnimationManager();
    }

    this.Update = function(deltaTime, context, deltaX, deltaY) {
        this.x -= this.velocity * deltaTime;

    if(this.BoundingBox().Intersects(player.BoundingBox())) {
            this.DisposeEnemy();
        }
    }
}

Enemy.prototype = new AnimationManager;
```

2. The `Enemy` object makes use of a function known as `Intersects`, which determines if two rectangles have collided. In order to utilize this function, we will need to implement a new object known as `Rectangle`.

```
function Rectangle() {
    this.left = 0;
    this.top = 0;
    this.width = 0;
    this.height = 0;

    this.InitRectangle = function(left, top, width, height) {
        this.left = left;
        this.top = top;
        this.width = width;
        this.height = height;
```

```
        return this;
      }

    this.Intersects = function(rect) {
      if(this.left + this.width < rect.left)
        return false;

      if(this.top + this.height < rect.top)
        return false;

      if(this.left > rect.left + rect.width)
        return false;

      if(this.top > rect.top + rect.height)
        return false;

      return true;
    }
  }
```

3. For our next step, we will need to create a new instance of the `Enemy` object inside of the `Level` object, and we also need to position an enemy unit within the `Level` constructor.

```
this.enemy = new Object;

this.tileWidth = 0;
this.tileHeight = 0;

this.InitLevel = function(width, height) {

this.tileWidth = tile.width;
this.tileHeight = tile.height;

for(var i = 0; i < 50; i++)
{
this.tiles[i] = 1;
}

this.enemy['10'] = 'Enemy';

this.AddTile(width, height);
this.AddEnemy(width, height);

        return this;
    }
```

4. Now that we have an enemy positioned within our level, we need to add that enemy unit to the level. This is done through means of the `AddEnemy` function, which is as follows:

```
var x, y;

this.AddEnemy = function(width, height) {

for(var i = 0; i < this.tiles.length; ++i) {
if(this.enemy[i]){

        x = i * this.tileWidth + this.tileWidth / 2;
        y = height - this.TerrainHeight(i);

        if(this.enemy[i] == 'Enemy') {
new Enemy().InitEnemy(enemy_left, x - enemy_left.width / 2, y -
enemy_left.height, 7, 4, 4);
        }
    }
  }
}
```

5. The final part that is required is to load the enemy sprite sheet into the application inside of the `Main` object.

```
var enemy_left = new Image();
enemy_left.src = "textures/enemy_left.png";
```

How it works...

The Enemy object creates a new enemy object that represents an animated object similar to the player object. The `Enemy` object constructor takes in a texture parameter, as well as a 2D position, depth position, frame count, and frame rate parameters. The texture is a 2D sprite sheet, which is used to animate the enemy. The x, y, and z positions represent the position of the enemy on the canvas as well as the position of the enemy texture within the list of layers within the game. The frame count is used to determine how many frames make up the enemy sprite sheet and finally the frame rate dictates how many frames the enemy texture should be played each second.

The `update` function within the `Enemy` object is used to move an enemy object along the x axis and towards the player. The `update` function is also used to check for any collisions between the player and the enemy. If there is a collision then the enemy object that collided with the player is removed from the game and the player has part of their health deducted. Finally we use the prototype keyword to extend the functionality of the `AnimationManager` to the `Enemy` object.

This collision detection makes use of the `Rectangle` object, which checks whether or not two rectangles are overlapping and if so whether a collision has occurred.

Inside of the `Level` object, we declare and initialize a new enemy object array. Inside of the `Level` constructor, we then assign a position for a new enemy object to be drawn to.

This position is then stored inside of the enemy object array and passed into the `AddEnemy` function. This function loops through each tile within the levels tile array and then loops through the enemy object array and places the enemy at the position above the tile that it corresponds to.

The final code extract refers to loading the enemy sprite sheet texture into the application. This is done exactly as we previously did for each of the textures within the game. A new enemy image object was created within the `Main` object and an external path that shows the location of the enemy sprite sheet texture was passed to the image object in question.

Adding pickups (Must know)

To allow the player to do more than just jump and avoid enemies, this recipe will focus its attention on the implementation of collectible items known as **pickups**. These pickups will be similar to the idea of collecting coins in *Mario* or gold rings in *Sonic* and will contribute to the player's score and increase the sense of enjoyability, that is, how fun the game is.

How to do it...

1. In order to implement pickups into our application, we will follow the exact same steps we took when implementing enemies.

2. We start off by creating a new object that represents a pickup. We begin by creating the pickups object, which is as follows:

```
function Pickup() {

    this.InitPickup = function(texture, x, y, z, frameCount,
                      frameRate) {
    this.InitAnimationManager(texture, x, y, z, frameCount,
    frameRate);
        return this;
    }

    this.DisposePickup = function() {
        this.DisposeAnimationManager();
    }

    this.Update = function(deltaTime, context, deltaX, deltaY) {
        if(this.BoundingBox().Intersects(player.BoundingBox()))
        this.DisposePickup();
```

```
      }
    }

    Pickup.prototype = new AnimationManager;
```

3. The next step involves creating a new pickup array object within the `Level` object and filling this array with the positions of a number of collectible items, that is, pickups, inside of the `Level` constructor. Insert the following code at the top of the `Level` script:

```
this.pickup = new Object();

this.tileWidth = 0;
this.tileHeight = 0;

this.InitLevel = function(width, height) {
this.tileWidth = tile.width;
  this.tileHeight = tile.height;

  for(var i = 0; i < 50; i++) {
    this.tiles[i] = 1;
  }

  this.pickup['1'] = 'Berry';

      this.AddTile(width, height);
  this.AddPickup(width, height);

      return this;
}
```

4. We then need to implement a function that will draw each of the pickups to the canvas at the position specified within the pickup object array.

```
this.AddPickup = function(width, height) {

  var x, y;

for(var i = 0; i < this.tiles.length; ++i){

if(this.pickup[i]){
      x = i * this.tileWidth + this.tileWidth / 2;
      y = height - this.TerrainHeight(i);

  if(this.pickup[i] == 'Berry') {
```

```
new Pickup().InitPickup(berry, x - berry.width / 2, y - berry.
height, 6, 1, 1);
            }
        }
    }
}
```

5. The final step required to implement and draw a pickup to the canvas involves loading the necessary texture for the pickup into the `Main` object.

```
var berry = new Image();
berry.src = "textures/berry.png";
```

How it works...

The `Pickup` script creates a new pickup object that represents an animated object similar to the player object. The `Pickup` constructor takes in a texture parameter, as well as a 2D position, depth position, frame count, and frame rate parameters. The texture is a 2D sprite sheet, which is used to animate the enemy. The x, y, and z positions represent the position of the pickup on the canvas as well as the position of the pickup texture within the list of layered textures within the game.

Both the x and y positions are measured in pixels and the z position represents layer depth. The frame count is used to determine how many frames make up the pickup sprite sheet and finally the frame rate dictates how many frames the enemy texture should be played at each second.

The `update` function within the `Pickup` object is used to check for any collisions between the player and a pickup object. If there is a collision then the pickup that collided with the player is removed from the game and the player has part of their score increased. This collision detection makes use of the `Rectangle` object, which checks whether or not two rectangles are overlapping and if so states that a collision has occurred.

Inside of the `Level` object, we declare and initialize a new pickup object array. Inside of the `Level` constructor, we then assign a position for a new pickup object to be drawn to. This position is then stored inside of the pickup object array and passed into the `AddPickup` function.

This function loops through each tile within the levels tile array and then loops through the pickup object array and draws a pickup at the position above the tile that it corresponds to.

The final code extract refers to loading the pickup texture into the application. This is done exactly as we previously did for each of the textures within the game. A new pickup image object is created within the `Main` object and an external path that shows the location of the pickup texture is passed into the image object in question.

Adding sounds (Must know)

As another form of emersion within the game, we will look at introducing sound effects to the game. However, in order to implement sound we must first adjust our game framework to allow the loading and updating of audio files. In order to do this, we will take advantage of the HTML5 Audio API, which is compatible with the latest versions of each of the major web browsers such as Google Chrome, Internet Explorer, Firefox, and Opera.

How to do it...

This task will be one of the shortest within the book as most of the functionality required to load and buffer audio within our game will be provided by the HTML5 Audio API, which is compatible with each of the major web browsers.

1. We begin by loading the required audio file into the application by placing the following code inside of the `Main` object after we load in each of the game textures:

   ```
   var effect = new Audio("audio/sound.wav");
   effect.load();
   ```

2. The next step involves playing the audio, in this case, we will tell the audio to play when the player has collided with a pickup. This is done by placing the following code inside of the collision detection check within the `Pickup` object's `Update` function.

   ```
   if(this.BoundingBox().Intersects(player.BoundingBox())) {
   this.DisposePickup();
   effect.play();
   }
   ```

How it works...

We begin by creating a new audio object, which holds the audio effect that is played when the player collides with a pickup. The audio file is loaded into the audio object by specifying a path to an external file, in this case, a `.wav` file. This file is then loaded into the application through means of the HTML5 Audio API's `Load` function. This function is used to load the audio file into the application prior to the canvas being drawn so that it is available when we begin to play the game.

In order for the sound effect to play when we collide with a pickup, we make use of yet another HTML5 Audio function known as `Play`. This function is responsible for buffering and playing the audio file.

Creating a graphical user interface (Must know)

Finally, no game would be complete without a user interface to display the player's score and health. In order to do this we will need to adjust the game frameworks `draw` method to allow text to be drawn to the canvas as well as introduction a number of variables which monitor and update the player's score and health.

How to do it...

1. To begin with, we will introduce two new variables that hold the player's score and health at the top of the `Main` object.

```
var score = 0;
var health = 100;
```

2. Next, we will draw the user interface elements to the screen, these elements are used to represent the player's score and health. Inside of the object manager 's `Draw` function place the following code before the `drawImage` function call:

```
this.context.font = "30px Arial";
this.context.fillText("Score: " + score, 15, 50);
this.context.fillText("Health: " + health, 625, 50);
```

3. Inside of the `Enemy` object's `Update` function, we will decrement the player's health each time they collide with an enemy. To do this update the collision detection check with the following:

```
if (this.BoundingBox().Intersects(player.BoundingBox())) {
this.DisposeEnemy();
health -= 14;
}
```

4. We will also need to increase the player's score each time they collect a pickup. Therefore in order to do this we will need to update the collision detection check within the `Pickup` object with the following:

```
if (this.BoundingBox().Intersects(player.BoundingBox())) {
   this.DisposePickup();
   effect.play();
   score++;
}
```

5. Once you have completed these final steps, your game should look something similar to the following screenshot:

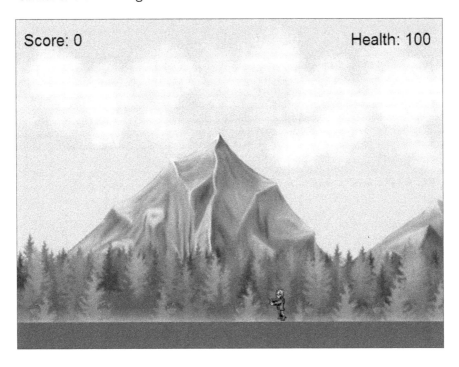

How it works...

We begin by creating two variables that are responsible for holding the player's score and their health.

The values of these variables are then drawn to the canvas through the use of string concatenation and the HTML5's `fillText` function that outputs text, with no effects applied to it, to the canvas.

Both of the score and health values are updated inside of either the `Enemy` or `Pickup Update` functions. The score value is incremented by one each time the player collides with a collectible object. Similarly the health value is decremented each time the player collides with an enemy object. Each of these values is updated in real time and the player's results are reflected on the canvas.

Finally, we perform a check to see if the player has collided with a pickup, that is, a berry, and if they have we play our sound effect and increment the score.

About Packt Publishing

Packt, pronounced 'packed', published its first book "*Mastering phpMyAdmin for Effective MySQL Management*" in April 2004 and subsequently continued to specialize in publishing highly focused books on specific technologies and solutions.

Our books and publications share the experiences of your fellow IT professionals in adapting and customizing today's systems, applications, and frameworks. Our solution based books give you the knowledge and power to customize the software and technologies you're using to get the job done. Packt books are more specific and less general than the IT books you have seen in the past. Our unique business model allows us to bring you more focused information, giving you more of what you need to know, and less of what you don't.

Packt is a modern, yet unique publishing company, which focuses on producing quality, cutting-edge books for communities of developers, administrators, and newbies alike. For more information, please visit our website: www.packtpub.com.

Writing for Packt

We welcome all inquiries from people who are interested in authoring. Book proposals should be sent to author@packtpub.com. If your book idea is still at an early stage and you would like to discuss it first before writing a formal book proposal, contact us; one of our commissioning editors will get in touch with you.

We're not just looking for published authors; if you have strong technical skills but no writing experience, our experienced editors can help you develop a writing career, or simply get some additional reward for your expertise.

Responsive Web Design with HTML5 and CSS3

ISBN: 978-1-84969-318-9   Paperback: 324 pages

Learn responsive design using HTML5 and CSS3 to adapt websites to any browser or screen size

1. Everything needed to code websites in HTML5 and CSS3 that are responsive to every device or screen size

2. Learn the main new features of HTML5 and use CSS3's stunning new capabilities including animations, transitions and transformations

3. Real world examples show how to progressively enhance a responsive design while providing fall backs for older browsers

HTML5 Games Development by Example: Beginner's Guide

ISBN: 978-1-84969-126-0   Paperback: 352 pages

Create six fun games using the latest HTML5, Canvas, CSS, and JavaScript techniques

1. Learn HTML5 game development by building six fun example projects

2. Full, clear explanations of all the essential techniques

3. Covers puzzle games, action games, multiplayer, and Box 2D physics

4. Use the Canvas with multiple layers and sprite sheets for rich graphical games

Please check **www.PacktPub.com** for information on our titles

WebGL Beginner's Guide

ISBN: 978-1-84969-172-7   Paperback: 376 pages

Become a master of 3D web programming in WebGL and JavaScript

1. Dive headfirst into 3D web application development using WebGL and JavaScript.

2. Each chapter is loaded with code examples and exercises that allow the reader to quickly learn the various concepts associated with 3D web development

3. The only software that the reader needs to run the examples is an HTML5 enabled modern web browser. No additional tools needed.

HTML5 Canvas Cookbook

ISBN: 978-1-84969-136-9   Paperback: 348 pages

Over 80 recipes to revolutionize the web experience with HTML5 Canvas

1. The quickest way to get up to speed with HTML5 Canvas application and game development

2. Create stunning 3D visualizations and games without Flash

3. Written in a modern, unobtrusive, and objected oriented JavaScript style so that the code can be reused in your own applications.

Please check **www.PacktPub.com** for information on our titles

www.ingramcontent.com/pod-product-compliance
Lightning Source LLC
LaVergne TN
LVHW080106070326
832902LV00014B/2446